as if

as if

E.D. BLODGETT

THE UNIVERSITY OF ALBERTA PRESS

THE UNIVERSITY OF ALBERTA PRESS

Ring House 2

Edmonton, Alberta, Canada   T6G 2E1

www.uap.ualberta.ca

Copyright © 2014 E.D. Blodgett

LIBRARY AND ARCHIVES CANADA CATALOGUING IN PUBLICATION

Blodgett, E. D. (Edward Dickinson), 1935–, author

    As if / E.D. Blodgett.

(Robert Kroetsch series)

Poems.

Issued in print and electronic formats.

ISBN 978-0-88864-727-6 (pbk.).—ISBN 978-0-88864-824-2 (epub).

—ISBN 978-0-88864-825-9 (Amazon kindle).—

ISBN 978-0-88864-823-5 (pdf)

    I. Title. II. Series: Robert Kroetsch series

PS8553.L56A85 2014   C811'.54   C2013-906917-8

                                               C2013-906918-6

First edition, first printing, 2014.

Printed and bound in Canada by Houghton Boston Printers,

Saskatoon, Saskatchewan.

Copyediting and proofreading by Peter Midgley.

A volume in the Robert Kroetsch series.

The University of Alberta Press is committed to protecting our
natural environment. As part of our efforts, this book is printed on
Enviro Paper: it contains 100% post-consumer recycled fibres and is
acid- and chlorine-free.

The University of Alberta Press gratefully acknowledges the support
received for its publishing program from The Canada Council for
the Arts. The University of Alberta Press also gratefully acknowledg-
es the financial support of the Government of Canada through the
Canada Book Fund (CBF) and the Government of Alberta through
the Alberta Multimedia Development Fund (AMDF) for its publish-
ing activities.

Canada

tibi

Die Musik kennt kein Nein.
— Robert Musil

I

as if by chance a book
had opened on your lap

a book that told of rain
falling and falling on

such small japanese towns
of rain falling through

the pines on ponds and where
the gravel gardens stood

their outlines fading so
that anything that passed

there was soon absorbed
small explosions of

the birds gone without
a trace into the air

and there were pictures in
the book that held within

its pages things that were
so bare they seemed composed

of light and air and trees
that had been honed into

simplicities that were
so ancient that if you

so much as picked them up
you would barely know

what they might have been
so gently do they rest

against your skin their warmth
an embrace that holds

all of you in light
the air of breathing trees

turning the page is not
as simple as it seems

colours begin to fade
where there had been rain

its memory is all
that hangs upon the air

and something stands between
you and where your gaze

turns on the empty sky
and what you thought you might

have seen shimmers before
you all beauty but

a kind of breathing that
takes up and gives away

how can music tell
the edge where silence ends

a colour that appears
of a sudden at

the corners of your eye
as one might pluck a string

in darkness and a sun
of music might spring up

the echo of it all
along horizons of

every living thing
rain and tree and air

whatever they are
they sing themselves in one

I am of colours that
no one can recall

and music fades into
a second silence more

profound than what had come
before without the pitch

of music that might say
what silences had been

unaccountably
the book slips from your lap

and you look up to see
that you are sitting by

a window gazing at
reflections on the glass

unable to discern
where you are among trees

your gaze rising up
upon the glassy air

as smoke over snow
or snow over smoke

and so you have become
a landscape or the way

one remembers them
as they come to mind

so many landscapes all
at once moving through

themselves and now and then
the sea along a beach

where orchards stand beneath
the wind and rising from

the water fish among
their roots rising against

the surface to take the sun
with them out of sight

how can you tell as you
are gazing through the glass

if it is not the shape
of memory you see

and whose it is if not
yours then what perhaps

I remembered and
passed along to you

a tree you never saw
that now takes its place

among the other things
that you recall that rise

before your eyes as what
the light in passing holds

as if there could be no
other memory

a tree invisible
remembering itself

and all the trees from which
it sprang green and full

of centuries of trees
standing in themselves

and so the shade where you
have walked is several shades

its hues a music that
falls slowly through

silence that expands
music and silence a

kind of space where trees
exhale their twilights through

the air mottled where
the sun comes and goes

its presence in the sky
disguised and bearing no

cadence to mark the fall
of shades or leaves or time

sometimes clouds as dusk
rises beneath the moon

take on the shape of sails
that pause upon their far

horizons casting shades
on the sea their shadows as

they float past a part
of all the shades that fall

from trees and all the shades
that rise at night to roam

uncertain through the air
darkness in their eyes

birds are in their wakes
intermittent in

the waves and in the dark
shades of themselves that are

what fates look like when they
are in the full pitch

of flight eternities
enfolded in their wings

the loneliness of stars
is not contained within

your book that lies upon
your lap and unconcerned

they turn through the night
their light unable to

enlighten the small things
that move beside us in

the dark nor us who seek
the way unknown to go

all of us left behind
in mysteries too deep

as if we were to take
a stone within our hands

and ask of it what is
the what of what it is

so the stars are
so stubborn through the night

turning through the space
of dark eternities

and right before your eyes
where all the world that you

can see moves past
the window where you sit

reach out and you can touch
the whole of night and stars

if you were blind you would
possess knowledge there

beneath your fingers stars
and where they have come from

but stars were not made
for us to gaze upon

their veiled timidities
perhaps a cat almost

asleep and sheltered from
the rain is able to

pretend that all that might
pass between himself

and stars has passed without
the least awareness shared

but wisdom like a star
rises in her eyes

but for us the most
oblique look does not

always lead us where
wisdom rises so

the nearest we might come
is in the play of shades

filtered by the trees
a play so rapid we

cannot be sure from what
unknown heaven of

the heavens light from what
we cannot see comes forth

no other wisdom is
given us but what

happens that we are not
always able to see

and trees can only lead
us where the stars are not

what our eyes can see
but feel as if we were

a cat almost asleep
our skin breathing air

naked and open then
our dreams not turning in

our minds but lying beside
us waiting for the rain

the stars about to appear
but what dreams are we

ready to receive
their movement in us so

stealthy there is no cat
that can keep pace with them

what is it that we see
unless it is what we

cannot see that shapes
what we think we see

sunrise behind a ridge
of distant mountains or

the wind that stirs the grass
what must have been the breath

of god that trees exhale
and we unthinking breathe

how birds come slowly home
and turn in circles round

their nests calling to
each other the air filled

with songs that sometimes pierce
the dim air and some

that float languidly
following their flight

round and over their nests
try as we might we are

not able to tell the birds
apart no matter how

slowly they fly nor can
we trace the paths they take

there is a mind they share
whose dreams they follow so

surely but what it thinks
is not other than

this dance and song of birds
together making one

idea that is of them
a movement that cannot

be stopped a movement that
is their portion of

grace we are given to see
without seeing at all

but grace invisible
is all that one desires

to see or hear or touch
without knowledge of what

it is wherever it
should fall through air or through

the barest outlines of
something we forgot

but comes insistently
as we might gaze upon

a quiet pond and see
shapes beneath its surface

that may be fish or may
be something yet unknown

like wakes invisible
that must follow them

like fire when it goes out
a falling leaf is full

of its fall as it slips
from its branch to begin its slow

descent floating on
the buoyant air toward

the ground there to rest
what is this fullness that

is and is not the leaf
the buoyancy of its

utter abandon to air
that holds and does not prevent

its falling toward the earth
gift giving up

a leaf that falls again
in you and when you wake

at night the echo of
it resonates against

the mind's ground as if
its autumn could not end

II

at other times you wake
and wonder when it was

when this might have occurred
the fall of one leaf

you might have been beside
a window reading a book

and looking up you see
it fall falling through

the words you just read
of someone living in

a desert where there were
no trees no leaves to fall

how great the leaf would be
overwhelming the book

where across the emptiness
leaves never fell

or you might glance again
and see your leaf against

the ground an agèd hand
still holding the light

the thought of it not one
but many pooling in

the mind the leaf in all
its phases traced upon

the sky as if it were
another face of the moon

but sitting under stars
almost inaudible

a leaf through darkness falls
and close to sighing it

settles on the ground
what sighs if not the dark

the air like a sad bride
giving way before it

perhaps it strikes a stream
unresistant to

the flow of water that
carries it beyond sight

perhaps to nestle for
a while where lilies grow

always homeless in
its fall but always held

a gift of water and
the air possessed by none

so this is what the leaf
must be passing through

but how it stays without
awareness in the mind

as if eternity
in passing came to rest

by instants there before
something carries it

away into the next
eternity to come

what else then is the leaf
if not a psalm that you

might speak moving through
the seed-time and harvest of

your voice with a pace
that cannot be reversed

at the centre a
certain poise that

without impatience waits
for each syllable

to fall where it cannot
fail floats upon

your breath that comes and goes
and chanting comes again

we do not know how we
have reached this point beneath

the stars or what has led
us our uncertainty

all we have to guide
us now perhaps to read

the stars as they spread out
upon the waters at

our feet their clarity
disturbed by wind and wave

but clarity's not a guide
or order or design

the grace we want to see
does not arrive as things

standing in the sun
not even trees but what

the trees bring with them of
unaccounted years

the rings of trees that have
long decayed before

our trees were known by us
in what dust do they

hide their grandeur as motes
turning through shade

and what you ask is our
dust that floats beside

us out of sight but us
as we have been through all

seed-times and harvests of
the past we cannot know

if not the greater psalm
that we walk through as lone

palmers along a way
that leads deeper into

a kind of rhythm that
shapes us as a dance

how lightly over the earth
through seed-time and all

harvests have the feet
of those who cannot be known

to us trodden in
their dance following steps

that came to them as waves
that move across a stream

the water of it without
awareness of the mind

impelling it the leap
of waves never at rest

and so it is that in
the leaf the star the tree

joy is not to be seen
but every turn they take

are shapes of alleluias
that rush though the air

birds lie upon
them passive partakers of

their huge buffets that
sweep them to the poles

ants around their nests
are no more intricate

in all the steps they take
steps that count time

filling the density of
centuries in their path

as if time were but
a choreography

of all that is but is
unseen and taking up

residence in us
remembering itself

imagine then a psalm
that playing over you

sings you into sleep
the voices that you hear

voices of them that sing
in tongues unknown to you

or anyone and in
a rhythm never felt

dancing over your flesh
and so it is that we

embracing are embraced
by these archaic songs

that are the murmurs of
forests enclosed by night

the whole naked world
dancing toward the stars

and upward from the streams
hills and mountains rise

followed by the great
anagoge of birds

reaching for the clouds
and after for the stars

the larger psalm of the earth
lifting as if against

the rain toward the place
it thinks its fullness took

its large departure up
beyond the sun and moon

from what unsounded well
of silence did the first

syllable begin
to speak declaring that

the reign of silence was
no more eternal but

the measure only of
the psalm as it laid out

a universe of what
was quick and what was dead

the second syllable
was found by passing birds

as if it were a seed
that fell at random from

the great silence of our
primordial desire

a seed unnoticed that
carried in itself

seeds of the whole psalm
that overwhelmed the air

how ancient yet it seems
daily newly sprung

spreading out in time
and simultaneously

collapsing time into
the moment of each word

as it is uttered the air
coming always toward

us asking us to breathe
inhaling all that has been

no one is capable
of holding all of what

is past and so we sigh
letting it escape

strange exchange of all
the air that everyone

has breathed with animals
and trees and creatures we

cannot imagine each
taking and giving of air

turning round us in its
invisibility

the gift that all must share
and leading us in that

dance that all perform
making us kin to stars

how near then are stars
beside us in the sun

not to be seen but known
as we would know a bird

that we have never heard
perched on the topmost branch

in that country where we
have never trod the ground

singing fragments of
the great psalm that he

has heard the hearing of
it enough for him to know

singing it was what he was
and what he was to be

what is the song but our
memory of all

that is past and all that is
given back and forth

the place where giving gives
and taking in return

takes only to pass
somewhere on into

the place where giving has
not been remembering

what yet will be and we
become the giving past

and so it is a song
composed of its refrains

where our burdens rest
in their eternities

burdens that are known
and joyously passed on

by all the singing beasts
our festival theirs

who has heard the stones
and how are they to be

sung lying beneath
the sun forgotten and

left as sterile seeds
stones that are the endless

wearing away of time
becoming sand and dust

stones that are the rest
of mountains standing in

the sun the rain the snow
their refrains refrains

of silence first and last
and of memory

the larger memory
the gift where all sleeps

III

and so we are as if
before music where

silence cannot be
measured unpossessed

by the time that we keep
boundless silence that

that does not know of stars
or where the seas end

here we must pause
not possible to say

what it is when we
imagine where it seems

to be at rest upon
horizons that are not

far from us but not
so near we might pretend

it is a tree among
other remembered trees

who could have dreamt of this
great rising of

silence that does not
belong to music we

might sing but in
its own rising stands

a voice that singing moves
in pitches we cannot

discern and if we were
to try approaching its

unsounded silence our
voices would return

to us without response
as if nothing could

speak of our awe
beyond the sudden gasp

that one might make if one
were found alone among

the stars with nothing beside
one but the stars and stars

are we born for this
to move in this place

where memory seems to fail
leaving us to turn

in darkness where there is
no unexpected light

where immobility
cannot be reached by time

were we born for this
we were born to be amazed

to gaze forever toward
beauty that cannot

be fathomed standing in
barely visible

veils of morning mists
upon its highest height

the sun careful in
its matutinal awe

almost turning away
ashamed almost to reveal

so how are we to gaze
unswervingly at this

overwhelming light
that it takes up and passes off

as if indifferent to
whatever heaven might

pour upon it as if
heaven itself were at

its prayers unable to
look elsewhere in its praise

but we are not the sun
and if we are to see

the holiness that we
might share unthinking with

the sun blindness would be
all we might expect

and so we must pretend
and say that what we see

this mountain that we claim
to see is nothing more

than that mountain that
stands at the world's edge

but the mountain that
we are not given to see

where is it and where
does it rise lifting its

silence into the air
that we breathe in and out

oblation that we share
even with the sun

is there a memory
beyond what we possess

a memory that speaks
inaudibly to ours

as one might stare transfixed
across a sea at night

and see the moon appear
upon the water and

the sky the same moon
but in another guise

rising so in dreams
you cannot tell the moons

apart so closely do
they seem to be the same

then the sea itself
appears to be a dream

except for the soft fall
of waves lapping your feet

but in the dream the sound
becomes a soft refrain

music merging so
you dream you are awake

then a silence we
cannot conceive comes in

to us a silence that
does not come before

or follow music but
is silence nothing else

silence resting on
the far horizon as

the silence of stones alone
full of knowledge that

undisclosed in their
quiet keeping lies

but stones cannot be ours
giving us only the

silence that they are
a silence that they share

with the great mountain where
in its being they

lie as if they lay
upon the memory

of all remembered things
in their keeping we

must lie without the least
of our knowing how

how can we then presume
to think that when we gaze

upon the mountain we
have seen it as it is

but we are drawn to it
as one might wish to hide

in what remembers us
imagining what we see

the mountain from its fog
emerging there to become

all the horizon that
we have to contemplate

the mountain barely to
be seen at evening when

the sun goes out of sight
the moon not enough

perhaps this is why the gods
have cultivated all

the mountains of the world
splashing through the springs

of their divinity
laying wisdom down

beside them as clothes
that cover their desire

light that we might see
fire from waterfalls

this is that light
that is reflected from

the mountain's flank that we
behold as mere light

the sun that seems to spread
another light upon

the rocks the hidden pools
bright autumnal trees

but what is at the end
of that horizon which

the mountain is if not
the line that passes through

the centre of the world
the shadow where the day

meets the dark and where
sowing and reaping pause

the shadow where the psalm
of psalms begins its chant

the shadow dance against
the air of all that breathes

the mountain that we are
unable to behold

the nothing that appears
to be a line that is

invisible a line
that ends only in

itself a line that is
a chanting psalm that is

always beginning as
a universe that is

always where the sigh
of all afflatus begins

under the slightest breath
of wind the snow lifts

across the white cape
that lies upon the crest

no other sign of time
but the coming and

the going of snow to mark
the slow turning of

the seasons coming back
refrain for departing suns

but what music is this
falling with the snow

across unfailing light
that breathes into the sun

light that is the all
of what we see when we

gaze beyond the stars
uninvented light

that neither rises nor
sets a light without

an orb to carry it
or place where it might be

the mountain then that we
think we see is of

that music and light
ungraspable upon

its uttermost ridge
where clouds come to rest

as if they were a kind
of aureole that we

looking upon it are sure
that we have seen god

but god that is enclosed
in that psalm that is

beyond hearing where
the is of all that is

rests inside its snow
the only knowledge it

imparts standing in
the ocean of its light

where through the air that moves
across it a leaf is to

be seen seeming to fall
a small breath beneath

it that is just enough
to hold it where it is

and if you turn away
you will see it still

moving slightly up
and then slightly down

our breath in consonance
dancing across the light

a cat's-paw that plays
sleepily over it